NEW ADVENTURES IN

BEADING EARRINGS

by

Laura Reid

Eagle's View Publishing Company
6756 North Fork Road
Liberty, UT 84310

ISBN: 0-943604-18-4

FIRST EDITION

TABLE OF CONTENTS

ACKNOWLEDGMENTS

Special thanks to:

Bonnie who planted the seed for this book;

Molly for making the work easy;

My husband Michael and sons Sean and Bridger for their
support; and,

My publisher, Monte Smith for his encouragement, to R. L.
(Smitty) Smith for his illustrations, to Deon DeLange for
inspiration, and to Brenda Martin for proofing, suggestions
and variations.

ABOUT THE AUTHOR

Laura Reid has been a professional crafts woman for over ten years. She first learned bead work from an ancient Indian woman she met in South Dakota twenty years ago.

Since that time, she has increased her knowledge and experience in bead work and leather crafts, and mastered other old time craft skills. These crafts continue to inspire her to create new and innovative items.

Presently, she lives in Northern Idaho, where she is currently working on new bead and leather projects and her second book.

INTRODUCTION

This book is unique and the original bead work designs are created for either the new or experienced crafts person. These new earring designs are meant to stimulate the creativity in each reader, with the purpose of making something special, beautiful and uniquely different, as well as being fashionable. Beaded earrings can be profitable or they can be personal treasures or special gifts. In any case, they are easy to make and fun to create.

All of these new designs are concerned with shape and form. Each section includes a different beading technique that is explained in easy-to-understand terms with helpful diagrams that are also easily followed.

You can change the colors to suit your own personal taste and by using different kinds of beads, create many variations of the designs themselves. The possibilities can be endless and exciting.

This book contains earrings of unusual shapes; they are simple to construct and not time consuming. It also includes a few earrings that are slightly more complicated and require more time to complete. For other beautiful earrings made with unusual materials and exciting forms, see my book *Adventures in Creating Earrings*..

* * * * *

Creating beautiful earrings is very rewarding. To make certain they are the best they can be, each project is detailed in instructions and graphic diagrams are included as a further guide. Also, after completion of each project are the directions for the finishing touches. This will insure a more perfect product. So, to begin there are several things to keep in mind that will make your bead work more successful:

(1)   Because these designs are concerned with shape and form, it is extremely important that the beads you use be uniform in size. Be careful in selecting both the bugle and seed beads. Bugle beads should be examined for broken ends and different lengths or widths; seed beads should be selected that are fairly even in size. This will insure evenness in the designs. In most packages or hanks there will be some irregular size beads and these should always be discarded.

(2)   Size 3/0 bugle beads may be used with Size 11/° or Size 12/° seed beads. Size 2/0 bugle beads may be used with Size 12/° seed beads. Remember, concerning seed beads, the larger the number, the smaller the bead. You will also be using larger than normal bugle beads for many of the designs and Size 10/° seed beads will do nicely with those.

(3)   To store and organize beads, the author uses microwave "TV dinner" trays. They are made of plastic, have 3 or 4 compartments and are very shallow. Beads in hanks or packages may be stored in the large portion, and loose beads can be placed in the smaller compartments. The loose beads are easily picked up

by the beading needle because the trays are so shallow; these trays also stack nicely. Saucers or other shallow trays can be used.

(4) When purchasing beads make certain you have enough to finish the project. Often the dye lots of beads will be different and hard to match up.

(5) The thread used in all of the projects is NYMO (nylon) beading thread. Size A is used for the smaller bugle and seed beads, or where many passes need to be made between beads. Size AA may also be used. Size B is used for the larger beads or where only a few passes are necessary.

The length of thread should always be at least 2 1/2 yards long before beginning the work. The tail-end thread should measure at least 6" to 8" long, so that there will be plenty of room to put a needle on it and work back through the bead work. Keep the tail-end thread taut, as well as the beading thread, as this will aid in handling the work and in maintaining the design as it forms. It is also a good idea to reinforce each step as it is completed by running the needle through the beads again in order to keep the design in shape.

A single thread is used in all projects and, as it is nylon, there is some stretch to it and can be pulled up tightly and knotted securely.

Knotting the thread is made by using a simple overhand knot between the tail-end thread and the needle thread, or by looping the needle thread between two beads, passing the needle through the center of the loop and pulling it tightly as shown in Figure 1. The thread that is between two attached beads is referred to as a Junction.

Figure 1

Adding a new thread is done by simply using the loop method with the needle thread at a Junction point near the bead work in progress. In all cases, make the knots small and neat so that they do not detract from the beauty of the earring.

(6) The size of the beading needles used are either a Size 15/° English Beading Needle or even a Size 12/° English Beading Long Needle. The ones from England seem to be stronger; the needles from Japan or Taiwan, have more flexibility.

(7) One thing to remember while your work is in progress, is to move the beading needle up the thread often to avoid fraying the thread in the middle of the work.

(8) Your work area should be one that has a flat surface covered with cloth or felt, with plenty of room for bead trays and tools. It is also important that it be a well lighted area. A table lamp or clamp-on elbow style lamp would be an asset while doing this close work to avoid eye strain.

(9) Because these earrings are shapes, you need to take a few extra steps to make certain they maintain their form. By using super glue on the joints and applying clear fingernail polish over specified places, you can achieve a more perfect product. Read the glue instructions carefully being mindful to keep fingers away from the area you are gluing.

In order to keep repetition to a minimum, only the first few projects in the book include a description of how and where to apply super glue and/or clear fingernail polish to the joints. So, if you choose to start with a more complex project, be sure to familiarize yourself with these instructions.

In all cases, you can manipulate the shapes until they conform and then apply the setting materials. This should be done on a flat surface and on material that will not be damaged by a spot of the polish or the glue.

(10) For small earrings or earrings that have few beads, the ear wires that may be hooked closed do very nicely. The french hook ear wires look best when placed on larger style earrings or the ones that have a lot of beads.

* * * * *

Porcupine quills are used in a few of the designs, and can also be used in place of large bugles if desired. They can be purchased from Indian craft supply stores.

Sort out the quills that are long and uniform in size. Cut off the tips and ends. You can clean them by simply using warm soapy water and a cloth or paper towel and wipe them free of dirt and oil.

You can be certain of how much of the brown tip to cut off by first cutting off the very tip, putting a seed bead up to it and seeing how much of it goes inside the bead. If you cut too much off the tip, when threaded on against a seed bead and pulled up tight it will go over the seed bead and cause your work to look irregular. If too little is cut off, it will go inside the seed bead. It should fit next to a seed bead the way a bugle bead would, using the proper size of both.

To use, measure each one for the project intended and cut them to size, by cutting the white bottom portion only as the tips should have already been clipped or cut. When working with quills you can use a thimble and needle-nose pliers with which to put the needle through the quills; or, you may want to pass a larger needle through the white pitch inside the quill thereby making a larger space inside the quill for the needle to pass. In either case, go directly through the middle of the quill and not along the inside edge.

You can store the rest of the quills in cans, boxes or heavy plastic bags. The quills may be sorted into many different sizes for different projects and you can keep them separated by putting them in envelopes with the size written on the outside.

* * * * *

* * * * *

7

To make this book work for you and allow you to use your own creative expression, the following information may be helpful:

There will be some designs that you prefer to others. Select one project after reading the *Contents* or thumbing through the book until you find one that strikes your fancy. Gather the materials required. Then take a look at the legend and see if you like the color combinations. Carefully read through the directions a few times before you actually begin. By studying the pictures and illustrations you will be able to visualize the process. When you are ready to begin, read each step through. Do the work and leave it momentarily to read the next step thoroughly, then continue. This way you will feel more confident to begin and complete the project.

Complementary colors are as important in creating a beautiful set of earrings as in choosing the style you prefer. To get a different idea of color combinations, check out your own wardrobe. Perhaps you tend to focus on one color more than others. Some people also tend to look better with silver jewelry and others in gold, so you can place silver or gold colored beads next to those of your favorite color and choose a complementary color that looks good with these. When the project is completed, it will be a piece of jewelry with the proper color combination that is a beautiful matching accessory to the particular wardrobe selection you have made.

If you select a project that you wish to change, study the information on Foundations, Ear wire Loops and Dangles. Make a drawing of the project with the changes you would like to make and a special note of appropriate changes or adjustments in the instructions. This part of creating your own design can be exciting.

If your purpose is to create earrings to sell as a product, be mindful that each new season has its own particular color combination in fashion. By studying the newest fashion magazines or by going to clothing stores, you will notice those outstanding colors and will get ideas from there.

I hope you find these new innovative designs fun to make and as rewarding as I have. ENJOY.

THE BASICS

This section will call specific attention to the variations shown in this book for Foundations, Ear wire Loops and Dangles. By combining different variations with the earrings shown, new designs can be created.

FOUNDATIONS

The foundation is a row of beads to which other beads are attached. The foundation can be very simple or can be a variation from many beading techniques.

The FIRST STYLE of foundation is used in the first project section (Points) and is done by simply threading on a desired number of bugle and/or seed beads, then threading back through them to form a loop or circle as shown on *Pages 15* through *17*.

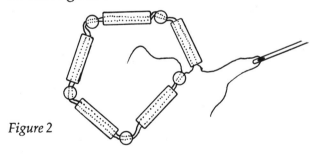

Figure 2

The SECOND STYLE of foundation is the bugle foundation and is shown on Page 21. It is made by threading on two bugle beads. A needle passes up through the first bead and down the second. A third bugle is threaded on, and the needle passes down through the second bugle and then up through the third. Another bugle is threaded on and the needle passes up the third and down the fourth. This process is continued until the desired number of beads is completed. Any number of bugle beads may be used in this foundation and it is important to go back through the work to strengthen it; in all of the designs, the thread will go back through the work and this is very important in holding the work secure.

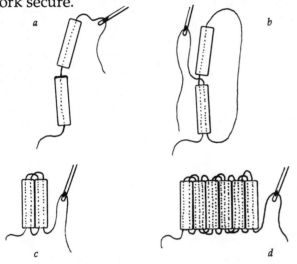

Figure 3

The addition of seed beads to the bugle bead foundation is done by threading on one seed bead and passing the needle between bugles 1 and 2 from the back to the front. To secure this bead, the needle will go back up through the seed bead only. Then another seed bead is threaded on and the process is repeated.

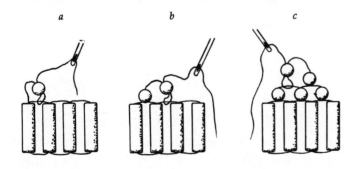

Figure 4

The THIRD STYLE is a variation of the bugle foundation and is shown on Page 25. This foundation is used to make the fans and the circle and is made possible by incorporating seed beads between the bugle beads. One bugle bead is threaded on, then a seed bead, then another bugle bead. The needle is passed up through the first bugle only, the beads pulled together tightly, then the needle passes through the seed bead and then down the second bugle bead. Another bugle bead is threaded on, then a seed bead. The needle passes down the second bugle and then up the third bugle, by-passing the second seed bead. Going back in reverse is done to strengthen the foundation.

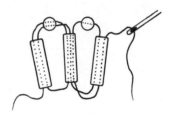

Figure 5

The FOURTH STYLE of foundation is made by using a straw as a form, using sets of bugle bead foundations and threading them together to create one piece from which other beads are attached.

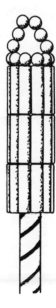

Figure 6

9

The FIFTH STYLE, is made with the peyote stitch. Almost any desired length may be made with the foundation. A certain number of beads is threaded on, and then gone back through to form a loop. A new bead is threaded on, going past one foundation bead and the needle passes through the next. So, it is a movement of going through every other one and this is continued for the desired length.

EARWIRE LOOPS

There are five styles of making the ear wire loops for the earring designs in this book and, while shown for specific earrings, are shown here:

STYLE #1 - You will come up through the appropriate seed bead, thread on the required number of beads, pass the thread through them again, and down the other side of the work, pulling the beads together tightly.

Figure 7

The beads used for placement of ear wire loops and dangles on the peyote stitch are referred to as Anchor Beads. This is a technique where the thread will go through one side of a certain bead and come out the other and through selected beads, then back again.

Figure 9

STYLE #2 - This style requires a certain number of beads threaded to sit on top of a bugle bead that is length wise.

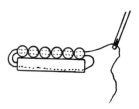

Figure 10

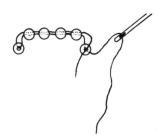

Figure 8

Then the needle passes through these seed beads until the middle two are reached. The needle comes out and the required number of seed beads are threaded on, gone through again to form a loop and then pass back through the center two seed beads, through the loop

10

again, then out through the remaining seed beads that lie on top of the bugle.

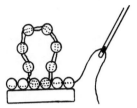

Figure 11

STYLE #3 - This style requires the use of anchor beads and is used with cylinder-style and peyote stitch earrings. A seed bead on one side, with another in line with it, is used by threading through it, threading on the number of seed beads required and then the needle passes over to the seed bead on the other side where the needle will go through it, then up and through the seed beads that form the loop. The needle then goes over and through the other side of the anchor bead and is knotted at a junction.

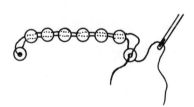

Figure 12

DANGLES

There are several new earring designs that include adding seed beads, bugle beads and/or quills for dangles. As there are many different styles of dangles, you can create a whole new earring look just by substituting one style for another.

STYLE #1 is made by threading on a single line, or strand, of seed and/or bugle beads, adding 3 seed beads to the bottom, and then taking the needle back through the beaded strand while skipping the last 3 seed beads.

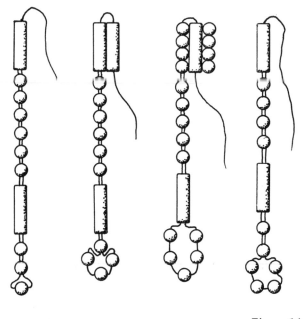

Figure 14

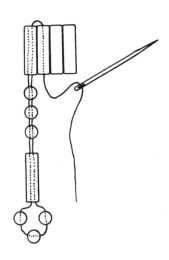

Figure 13

Then pass the needle through the foundation bugle or seed beads. By pulling the thread up with one hand and pulling the center bead of the last three with the other hand, the dangle will be tightened and straightened out. One thing to keep in mind is that the dangles should not be pulled up too tightly as they will be stiff and have no freedom to swing. Also, do not allow the dangles to hang too loosely as this would allow the thread to show. Shown below are four possible variations (see top right).

STYLE #2 is called a multi-loop. This is done by going down the first bugle, threading on the required number of beads, going across to the end bugle and up through it. Then work the needle back through the foundation to the first bugle, go down it, thread on the number of beads required (there will be more than the first loop to create a draping effect) then go back up through the end bugle.

Figure 15

12

To this second style, a third strand may be added with six or more beads for a variation.

choose to go back through, as shown below.

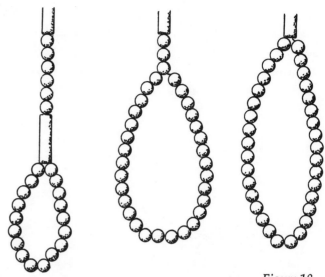

Figure 18

Figure 16

STYLE #3 is a straight loop dangle. Thread on the desired number of beads and then take the needle up through a bugle and the first few beads only.

Figure 17

This loop dangle can be lengthened or shortened depending upon the look that you prefer. You may increase or decrease the number of beads on the thread and/or where you

Other variations of these three styles may be used. Below are a few illustrations using Style #1: By adding a few more beads to each strand until reaching the center and then decreasing equally to the other side, you can create a "V" effect. By decreasing a few beads on each strand until you reach the center and then increasing by the same number, it will make an inverted "V" form.

Figure 19

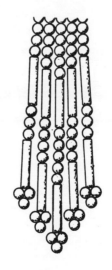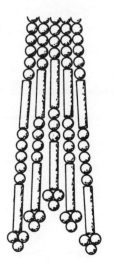

13

NOTES

POINTS STYLE EARRING

5 POINT STAR EARRING

Materials Required

Size "A" Thread
Size 15/° Beading Needle
Size 3/0 Bugle Beads (Brown)
Size 11/° Seed Beads
      Transparent Yellow
      Solid Yellow
      Transparent Red
Clear fingernail polish

Using the size "A" Thread (measuring 2 1/2 yards in length), thread on one bugle bead (keeping your thumb near the last six inches of the thread to keep it from slipping off). Add a seed bead. Continue alternating bugle and seed beads until you have five bugle beads and five seed beads on the thread. Meet the first bugle bead near your thumb and run the thread through all of the beads again. You have now formed the foundation of the Star (see *Figure 1*).

Pull the threads taut and tie them together in a knot. Leave the six inch tail-end thread to be worked back through the work later. Pass the needle through the first seed bead (do not go through the bugle bead). Thread on another seed bead, a bugle bead, then three seed beads. Pass the needle down through the second bead (see *Figure 2*), and pull the thread taut. Add one seed bead, one bugle, one more seed bead and pass the needle through the foundation bead (*Figure 3*). One star point has been completed. Repeat the instructions until there are five star points finished.

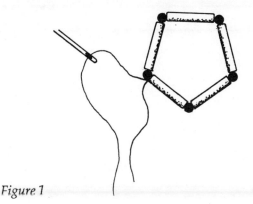

Figure 1

Figure 2

Figure 3

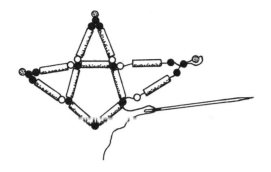

FINISHING

Figure 4

Now that it is almost completed, turn the earring around until it looks balanced and find the star point that looks like it should be the top one. Run your thread through the foundation again until you reach the left side of the star point you have chosen. Pass the thread up through to the first seed bead near the top and thread on six (6) seed beads. Pass the needle through the six beads again forming a loop for the ear-wire. As shown in *Figure 4*, pull the loop snug, then pass through the first seed bead on the right side of the star point (placing the ear-wire loop behind the point tip), and down into the foundation where you can tie a knot near the bugle and go back through the foundation, clip-

ping off the thread close to a bead.

Put the tail-end thread on the needle and pass it through a few of the foundation beads. Then clip off the excess thread.

The last step would be to lay the star down on a flat surface and brush a small drop of fingernail polish on all of the joints of the Star as

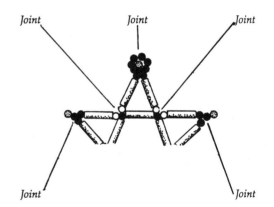

Figure 5

indicated on *Figure 5*. Allow to harden (4 to 6 hours).

5 Point Star Legend

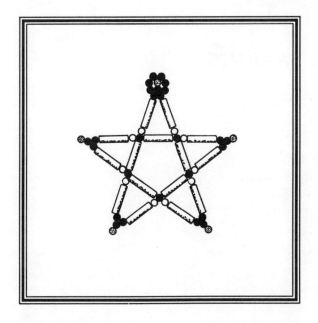

Legend

▭ Brown 3/0 Bugle Beads

● Transparent Yellow 11/° Beads

○ Solid Yellow 11/° Seed Beads

◉ Trans Red 11/° Seed Beads

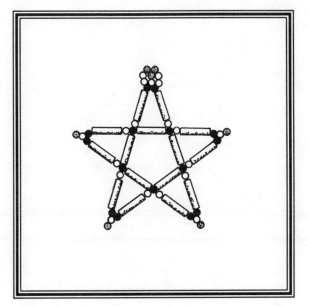

Variation

▭ Gold 3/0 Bugle Beads

○ Transparent Yellow 11/° Beads

● Solid Red 11/° Seed Beads

◉ Trans Red 11/° Seed Beads

SNOWFLAKE EARRING

Materials Required

Size "A" Thread
Size 15/° Beading Needle
Size 2/0 Lavender Bugle Beads
Size 11/° Seed Beads
    Pearl Light Blue
    Transparent Cobalt Blue
    Transparent Purple
Super Glue
Clear fingernail polish

As in the Star Earring (Pages 15 through 17), you will make the foundation for the snowflake first. Using the size "A" Thread (measuring 2 1/2 yards in length), thread on one bugle bead (keeping your thumb near the last six inches of the thread to keep it from slipping through the beads). Add a seed bead. Continue alternating bugle and seed beads until you have eight bugle beads and eight seed beads on the thread. Meet the first bugle bead near your thumb and run the thread through all of the beads again. You have now formed the foundation of the Snowflake (see *Figure 1*).

Pull the threads taut and tie them together in a knot. Leave the six inch tail-end thread to be worked back through the work later.

Take the needle through the next foundation seed bead. Thread on one seed bead, one bugle bead, one seed bead, three more seed

Figure 1

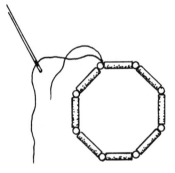

Figure 2

18

beads of another color (see Legend), and one more seed bead. Take the needle back through the second to last bead and pull the thread up tightly (as shown in *Figure 2*).

Add two seed beads that are colored to match the three on the left side of the point, then add one seed bead, one bugle bead, and finally the last seed bead. Take the needle through the foundation seed bead and repeat this step until all of the eight points are completed (*Figure 3*). It is a good idea to reinforce each point by running the needle through a second time.

When all eight points are finished, come back through the first seed bead you began with when you made the first point. (The points will not stay in place very well at this stage. Keep the thread taut and work with the points as best you can, knowing that when you add the seed bead in the following step, each point will stay in place.)

Take the needle up the left side of the first

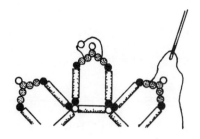

Figure 4

Figure 5

Figure 3

point and come out of the second seed bead, as shown in *Figure 4*. Thread on one seed bead and pass the needle down the second bead on the right side going through all of the beads back to the base seed bead; then continue up the left side of the next point to the same point and repeat this step until all eight points are completed. The one bead placed in the middle of the top point will fall smoothly into place by squeezing the top between your thumb and forefinger as

you pull the thread taut.

FINISHING

To finish the Snowflake Earring, straighten out the points and decide which one looks the best for centering and placement of the ear-wire loop. Go through the foundation again and come up on the left side of the point you have chosen. Take the needle up through the first seed bead, the bugle bead, and come out after three seed beads (*Figure 5*). Thread on eight seed beads. Thread through them again forming the loop in back of the point tip. Pull the thread taut, then pass the needle through the third seed bead on the right side and work your way down to the base and through the foundation seed bead.

Tie a knot between the seed bead and the bugle bead, go through a few more foundation beads and clip off the thread close to your work.

Now repeat this for the six inch tail-end thread.

Lay the work on a flat surface and drop a very small amount of super glue on each of the joints. Allow to dry. If you think the work could use extra strength, you may also brush finger-nail polish over the joints after the glue has been allowed to set for awhile.

Snowflake Legend

Legend

▭ Lavender 2/0 Bugle Beads

● Pearl Lt Blue 11/° Seed Beads

○ Trans Cobalt Blue 11/° Beads

◎ Trans Purple 11/° Seed Beads

Variation

▭ Royal Blue 2/0 Bugle Beads

○ Trans Yellow 11/° Seed Beads

● Trans Orange 11/° Seed Beads

◎ Trans Dk Red 11/° Seed Beads

CROSS EARRING

Materials Required

Size A Nymo Thread
Size 15/° Beading Needle
Size 3/0 Silver Green Bugle Beads
Size 11/° Seed Beads
       Transparent Dk Green
       Transparent Yellow
       Solid Light Green
Clear Fingernail Polish

The Cross Earring with tiny flowers in the top of each point is made by using a bugle bead foundation with four bugle beads. While making the earring, keep the *Legend* in mind so that you place the correct colored beads in the right place. The work procedes much easier if each step is reinforced as it is completed. For example, in *Step 1* when the bugle beads are brought parallel to each other, take the needle through each bugle again. This will help to keep each step in its proper place and maintain the shape of the design. Remember to keep both threads taut.

Step 1 - Using a single thread (just over 2 1/2 yards long), place two bugle beads on the thread and push them to within six inches of the

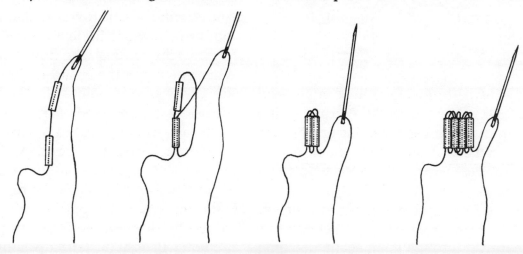

Figure 1

21

end (leaving enough tail-end thread to tie off later).

Holding the short thread down, make a clock-wise circle with the needle and go "up" through the first bugle bead following the direction of the thread. Pull the thread tight, and the two bugle beads will come together parallel with each other.

The needle will now be coming "up" through the first bugle bead. Complete this step by running the needle "down" through the second bugle bead. Continue adding bugle beads, one at a time, following this procedure until you have four bugle beads parallel to each other for the foundation, as shown in *Figure 1*.

Step 2 - When the foundation is completed, turn it upside down and on the long thread add one seed bead, one bugle bead, and six seed beads. Go back through the fifth seed bead and then thread on four seed beads, one bugle bead and one seed bead (*Figure 2*). Take

Figure 2

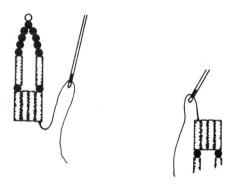

Figure 3

the needle down through the fourth bugle bead.

Step 3 - Now turn the earring upside down so that your thread is coming up out of the bugle bead on the left side as shown in *Figure 3*. Then repeat the instructions above to form the second point.

Step 4 - With the two points completed, as shown in *Figure 4*, strengthen them by running the thread through them again; this time,

missing the top two seed beads.

Step 5 - Now take the needle up to and through the left side of the first point and come out above the first seed bead after the bugle bead (*Figure 5*) where you will work the flower into the top of the point.

Figure 4

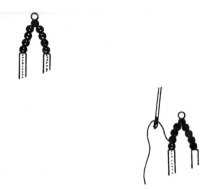

Figure 5

Step 6 - Thread on three seed beads (see Legend) and bring the needle down to and through the corresponding seed bead on the right side (see *Figure 6*). Add one seed bead, pass the needle through the center seed bead of the previous three seed beads, add one seed bead and pass the needle down through the bugle bead on the left side. Pull the thread taut and you have formed the first flower.

Step 7 - Take the needle straight down through the first foundation bugle bead, turn your earring upside down so that the thread is coming up through the left side and repeat *Steps Five* and *Six* to finish the flower in this point. When you finish, the thread should be at the left side of the second point and take it down and out below the first seed bead at the bottom (or just above the bugle bead). Turn the earring upside down so that the thread is still on the left.

Step 8 - Thread on one seed bead, one bugle bead, six seed beads and repeat *Step Two*. However, when this point is completed, take the needle through the first foundation bugle and you will be at the left side of this (the third)

22

Figure 6   *Figure 7*

point. Repeat *Steps Four, Five* and *Six*. When the flower in this point is finished, pass the needle up and down through the foundation bugle beads so that you can finish the final (fourth) point.

     Step 9 - Turn the work so that the thread is at the left side of the earring and repeat the steps necessary to finish this last point.

FINISHING

     Center the work and choose the point that looks best for the ear-wire loop. Take the needle back through the work and up the left side of this point until you reach the third seed bead from the top. Thread on eight seed beads,

go through them again so that they form a loop, and then take the needle down through the corresponding seed bead on the right side so that the loop is formed and held in place behind the beads at the tip of the point (*Figure 7*). Take the needle down the right side and form a knot that will be hidden between the beads. Then thread through the foundation and clip off the excess thread. On the six inch tail-end thread, tie a knot between beads and then thread this through the work and cut off any excess.

     Lay the Cross Earring on a flat surface and brush clear fingernail polish on the bugle base and on all of the joints. Allow four to six hours to dry.

(Legend on Page 24.)

Cross Earring Legend

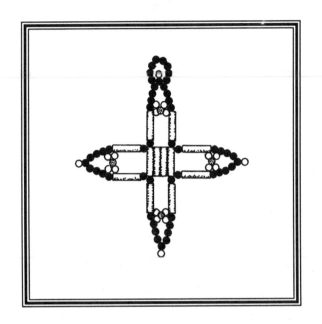

Legend

	Silver Green 3/0 Bugle Beads
●	Trans Dk Green 11/° Beads
◎	Trans Yellow 11/° Seed Beads
○	Light Green 11/° Seed Beads

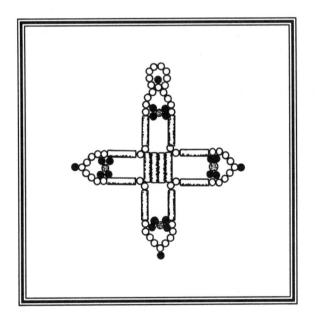

Variation

	Pink 3/0 Bugle Beads
○	Luster Red 11/° Seed Beads
◎	Trans Red 11/° Seed Beads
●	Iris Red 11/° Seed Beads

FAN STYLE EARRING

Steps 1 through 6 below will be used in this and the next four earring styles.

SMALL FAN EARRING

Materials Required

Size "A" Thread
Size 15/° Beading Needle
Size 3/0 Black Bugle Beads
Size 11/° Seed Beads
          Trans Dark Blue
          Gold
Super Glue
Clear Fingernail Polish

Figure 1

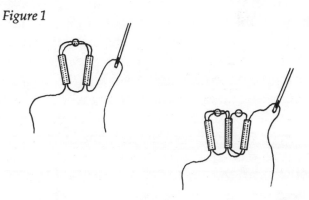

Figure 2

The foundation for the Fan Style Earring is a variation of the Bugle Bead Foundation shown in the Cross Earring. As you work, be sure and keep the *Legend* in mind so that the right color beads will be placed in the correct place. Also, remember to reinforce your bugle bead foundation as you build it.

Step 1 - With a single thread 2 1/2 yards long, thread on one bugle bead, one seed bead, and one bugle bead (*Figure 1*). Leave a six inch tail-end thread that is not taken through the beads. Take the needle back up through the first bugle bead and pulling the beads tightly together, pass the needle through the seed bead, then down through the second bugle bead.

Step 2 - The thread with the needle is now coming out of the bottom of the second bugle bead. Keeping the tail-end thread to the left of the work, thread on one bugle bead and one seed bead. Pass the needle down through the second bugle, pulling the beads together, and then up through the third bugle bead as shown

25

in *Figure 2*. The thread should be coming out of the top of the third bugle bead.

Step 3 - Thread on one seed bead and one bugle bead. Take the needle back up through the third bugle, then through the seed bead and down through the fourth bugle bead. Now repeat *Steps Two* and *Three* until you have ten bugle beads and nine seed beads in place as shown in *Figure 3*.

Figure 4

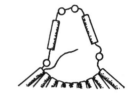

Figure 5

Figure 3

Step 4 - Threading back for strength, pass the needle up through the ninth bugle bead, then through the seed bead and down through the next bugle bead. Go up through the next bugle bead (thus skipping one seed bead), and continue in this manner. When the needle passes through the second bugle bead (in a down direction) tie a knot between the tail-end thread and the needle thread. Take the needle thread back up the second bugle, over and through the seed bead and down the first bugle bead. Turn the work upside down so that the fan part (with the seed bead separations) is at the bottom and the thread is at the top of the first bugle bead and to the left of the work. Leave the tail-end thread uncut for now (see *Figure 4*).

Step 5 - This step will create the fan handle. Thread on one seed bead, one bugle bead, two seed beads, one bugle bead and one seed bead and pass the needle down through the tenth bugle bead in the foundation (*Figure 5*). Go through the seed bead on the bottom and then up through the ninth bugle bead. Take the

needle back through the seed bead on top of the tenth bugle bead, through all of the beads of the handle, coming out at the bottom of the first bugle bead. Pass through the seed bead and up through the second bugle bead and back up through the first seed bead on top of the first bugle bead and continue through the top two seed beads (*Figure 6*).

Step 6 - To place the ear-wire loop, thread on six seed beads. Take the needle back around through the two seed beads and then up through the six seed beads again to strengthen the loop; then, continue through the seed beads (*Figure 7*). Pass the needle down the bugle bead handle and through the end bugle at the bottom so that the thread is at the right of the work. Now turn the earring upside down so that the thread is at

Figure 6

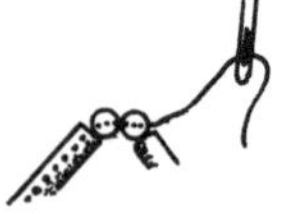

Figure 7

26

the right and the fan handle (with loop) is at the bottom.

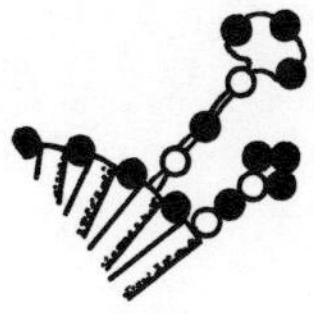

Figure 8

Step 7 - Now you want to add the lacy edging to the fan. The thread should be coming up out of the foundation bugle bead on the right. Thread on six seed beads and then take the needle back through the first three seed beads and all the way down through the bugle bead. Take the needle up through the next foundation bugle bead and repeat this step until all ten foundation bugle beads have the lacy edging on them (Figure *8*).

FINISHING

Tie a knot at the first bugle bead of the handle, then continue the thread through some more beads in the work and clip off the excess. Put the needle through the tail-end thread, pass through a few beads and cut it off. Pull the bottom of the fan down to get a nice shape.

Now glue the joints of the handle and the bottom line of beads that begin the lace part. Remember, as always, use a very small amount of glue to do this. Allow to dry completely. Then brush on clear fingernail polish in the same places for extra strength and allow four to six hours for this to dry.

Small Fan Legend

Legend

▭	Black 3/0 Bugle Beads
●	Trans Dk Blue 11/° Seed Beads
○	Gold 11/° Seed Beads

Variations

▭	Silver 3/0 Bugle Beads
●	Trans Black 11/° Seed Beads
○	While-Lined Red 11/° Beads

LARGE BUGLE FAN EARRING

The Large Bugle Fan Earring is a variation of the Small Fan Earring. In that you will be following some of the instructions from that earring, keep in mind the Legend (*Page 30*) shown with this earring.

Step 1 - Follow *Steps One* through *Seven* as described in the Small Fan Earring on *Pages 25* through *27*. However, before knotting, the needle should go through the seed bead at the beginning of the handle and turn the work so that the thread will be at the left side as shown in *Figure 1*.

Step 2 - Thread on one seed bead, pass the needle underneath the thread that is between the first and second bugle beads. Secure the bead by passing the needle back up through the seed bead only. Then thread on another seed bead and again secure underneath the thread that is between the second and third bugle beads and come up through the seed bead (*Figure 2*). Repeat across the top of the fan in this manner. Make sure that the seed beads are a bit smaller in diameter in order to fit smoothly across the top of the fan.

FINISHING

Finishing is done just like shown in the Small Fan Earring (*Page 27*).

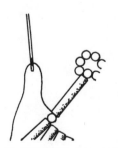

Figure 1

29

Figure 2

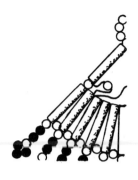

Large Bugle Fan
Legend

Legend

▭ Gold 5/0 Bugle Beads

○ Gold 10/° Seed Beads

● Luster Red 10/° Seed Beads

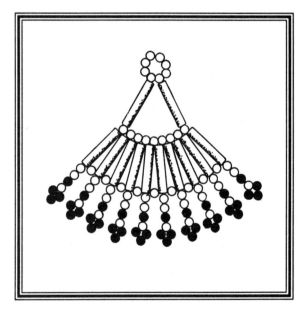

Legend

▭ Silver 7/8" Bugle Beads

○ Crystal 11/° Seed Beads

● Root Beer 11/° Seed Beads

LARGE AND SMALL BUGLE FAN EARRING

Materials Required

Size "A" Nymo Thread
Size 15/° Beading Needle
Size 3/0 Silver Bugle Beads
Size 4/0 Luster Blue Bugle Beads
Size 11/° Seed Beads
      Silver
      Blue
Super Glue
Clear Fingernail Polish

The Large and Small Bugle Fan Earring is a variation of the Small Fan Earring that is illustrated on *Pages 25* through *27*. In that you will be following some of the first instructions from that earring, keep in mind the *Legend* shown with this earring so that everything will be placed as planned.

Step 1 - With the thread measuring about 2 1/2 yards long, begin threading on eight bugle beads and seven seed beads between them following *Steps 1* through *6* of the Small Fan Earring on *Pages 25* thru *27*.

Step 2 - In place of the lacy edging (*Step 7* in the Small Fan Earring on *Page 27*), when *Step Six* has been completed (your thread should be at the right of your work coming down out of the last, or eighth, bugle bead with the fan "handle" to the top). Thread on three seed beads, one large bugle bead, five seed beads, one large bugle bead and three seed beads (see *Legend* for suggested colors). Pass the needle up through

Figure 1

the seventh bugle bead, and then over and down through the eighth bugle bead only. Then pass the needle through the seed bead that separates the eighth and seventh bugle beads, then down through the three seed beads and one bugle bead. Thread on five seed beads, one large bugle bead, three seed beads and then pass the needle up through the sixth bugle bead, pulling all of the beads up tightly, and then down through the seventh bugle bead. Take the needle through the seed bead that separates these bugle beads and down through the three seed beads and one large bugle. Repeat this step until all eight of the edges are completed (*Figure 1*).

FINISHING

Work the thread up to the top of your work and tie a knot at the first seed bead of the handle, go through some of the beads and then clip off the excess thread. Put the needle through the tail-end thread, pass this thread through some of the beads and cut off any excess. Pull the bottom of the fan down to get a nice shape. Glue the joints, the top of the fan, and the bottom line of seed beads that start the lacy edging. Allow the earring to dry completely and then brush on clear fingernail polish in the same places. Allow four to six hours to dry.

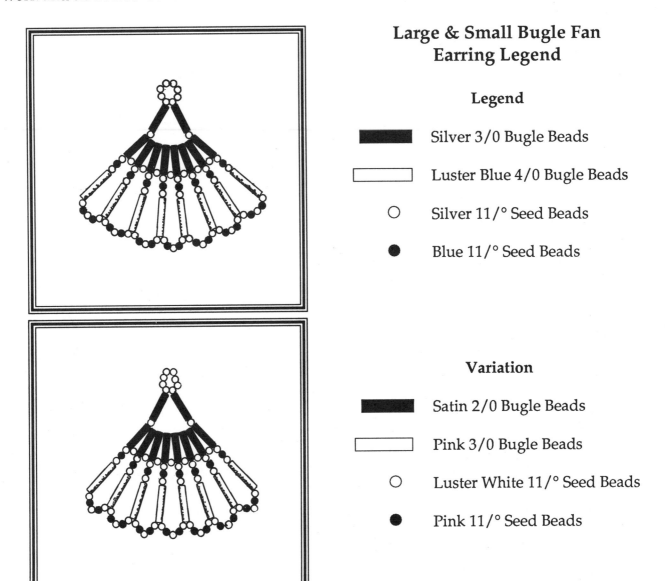

Large & Small Bugle Fan Earring Legend

Legend

▬	Silver 3/0 Bugle Beads
▭	Luster Blue 4/0 Bugle Beads
○	Silver 11/° Seed Beads
●	Blue 11/° Seed Beads

Variation

▬	Satin 2/0 Bugle Beads
▭	Pink 3/0 Bugle Beads
○	Luster White 11/° Seed Beads
●	Pink 11/° Seed Beads

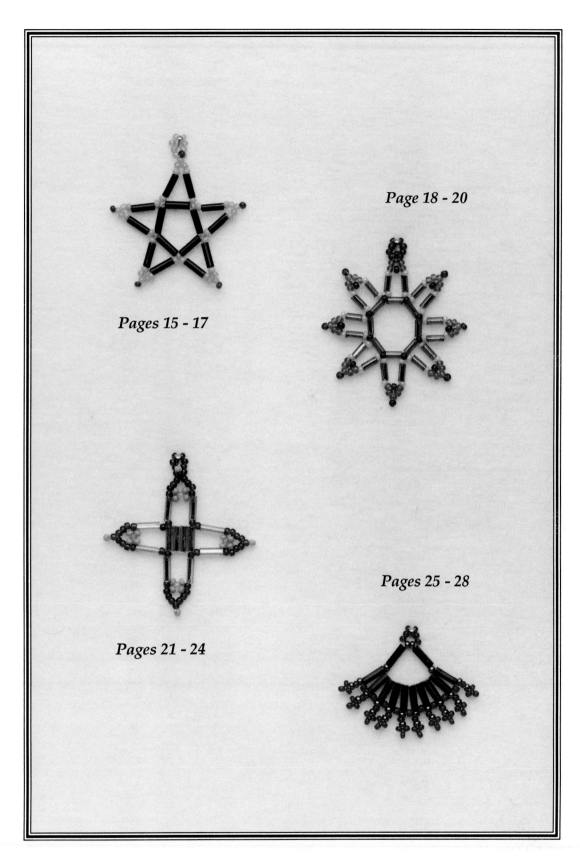

Page 18 - 20

Pages 15 - 17

Pages 25 - 28

Pages 21 - 24

PLATE I

Pages 29 - 30

Page 31 - 32

Pages 33 - 35

Pages 36 - 37

PLATE II

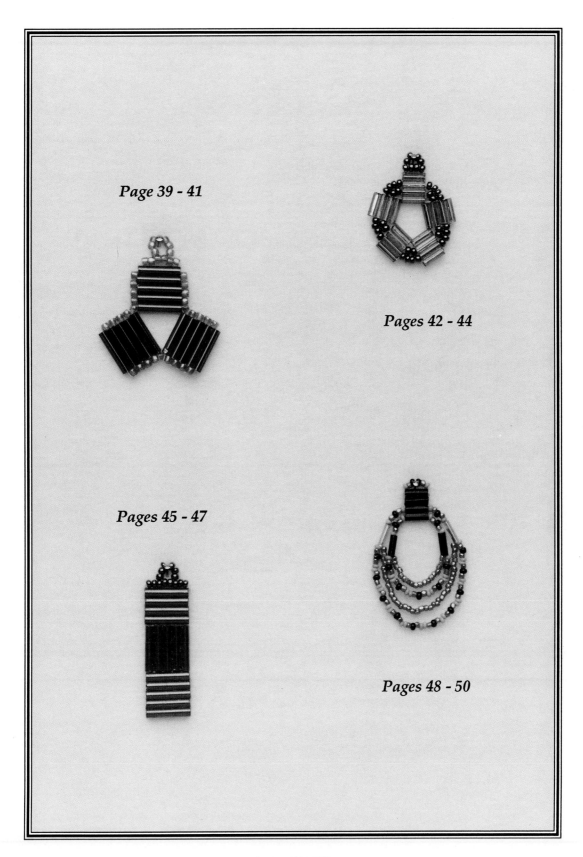

Page 39 - 41

Pages 42 - 44

Pages 45 - 47

Pages 48 - 50

PLATE III

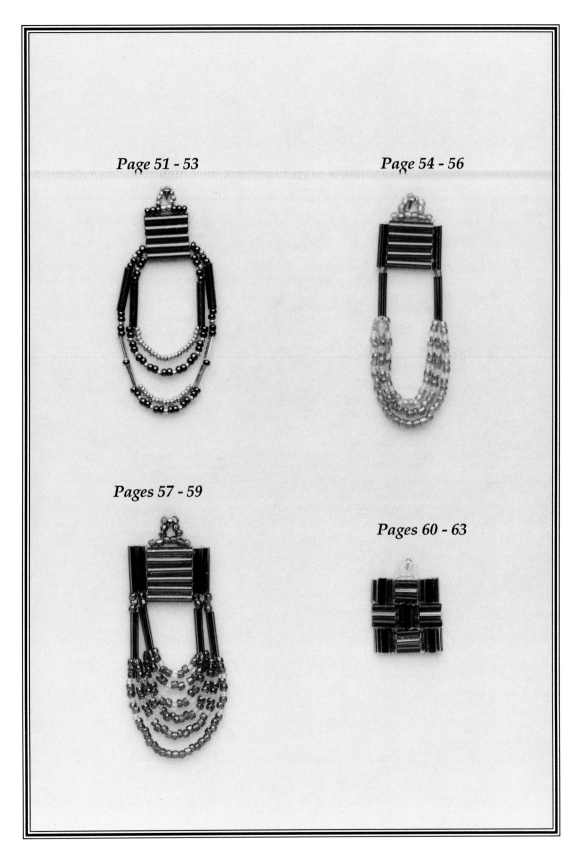

Page 51 - 53

Page 54 - 56

Pages 57 - 59

Pages 60 - 63

PLATE IV

QUILL FAN EARRING

Materials Required

Size "A" Nymo Thread
Size 15/° Beading Needle
Porcupine Quills
Size 10/° Silver Seed Beads
Size 11/° Red Seed Beads
Clear Fingernail Polish

This is a variation of the Small Fan Earring that is illustrated and explained on *Pages 25* through 27. However, in that the materials used are unique to this project, please read all of these instructions before beginning; you may also want to review the section on porcupine quills in the Introduction. Also, as you will be following the instructions from another part of this book, keep the *Legend* included with this project in mind as you work on these beautiful earrings.

Step 1 - Porcupine quills are available from many craft stores that specialize in Indian or "mountain man" crafts. Sometimes they are readily available next to highways and country roads.

After you have the quills, choose twelve that are the same diameter. Clean them well in a solution of soapy water and then allow them to dry completely; they will become hard again after they dry. After cleaning them, cut the brown tips slightly, measure about 1/2" and cut

them to size. Make sure that they are all exactly the same length.

Step 2 - Follow Steps One through Seven of the Small Fan Earring on *Pages 25* thru 27, substituting the quills for bugle beads and making sure that the brown quill tips are at the bottom of the fan as shown in *Figure 1*.

Figure 1

FINISHING

Finish off as in the Small Fan Earring (Page 27). Use clear fingernail polish on the joints of the handle and the top and bottom of the fan. Allow to dry thoroughly (about four to six hours).

OPTION ONE

You may want to work a row of seed beads, using the size 11/° noted in the *Materials Required* across the top of the fan as illustrated and explained in the Large Bugle Bead Fan on *Page 29*.

OPTION TWO

The Variation Legend with this project shows this same earring made by using Size 10/° Seed Beads, Size 3/0 Bugle Beads in the handle and Size 7/8" Bugle Beads in the fan. This option is shown to give you an idea of the many variations that are possible using the fundamentals given in this book.

Quill Fan Earring Legend

Legend

☐ Porcupine Quills

○ Silver 10/° Seed Beads

● Red 11/° Seed Beads

Quill Fan Earring Legend

Variation

▭	Emerald 7/8" Bugle Beads
▮	Silver 3/0 Bugle Beads (Handle)
○	Pearl White 10/° Seed Beads
●	Luster Green 11/° Seed Beads

CIRCLE EARRING

Materials Required

Size "O" Nymo Thread
Size 15/° Beading Needle
Size 3/0 Silver Bugle Beads
Size 10/° Crystal Teal Cut Seed Beads
Size 10/° Silver Seed Beads
Clear Fingernail Polish
Super Glue

Step 1 - The Circle Earring is a variation of the Small Fan Earring shown on *Pages 25* through *27*. In this case you will use twenty-four (24) bugle beads and twenty-four seed beads. The object here, after following *Steps One* through *Six* of the Small Fan Earring instructions is to form a circle. You close the circle by going down through the first bugle bead, then up through the next bugle and go back through the entire work again for strength. With this style, make sure that the thread on the outside is not too taut or the circle will form a cone.

Step 2 - The ear-wire loop can be made by simply threading on seven seed beads, going back through six of them for added strength, and then back down the first seed bead as shown in *Figure 1*.

FINISHING & OPTION

You may choose to go through the center of the circle and attach beads in the fashion explained in the Large Bugle Bead Fan (*Page 29*), using seed beads attached at every other space. If not, pass through the beads, tie a knot, go through more of the beads and then clip off the excess. Work the tail-end thread likewise. Lay the work down on a flat surface and glue the outside of the circle and then the inside. After the glue has dried, brush on clear fingernail polish in the same place and allow four to six hours to dry.

OPTION TWO

Another option is to use 2 seed beads between each bugle bead. This requires less bugle beads and you finish off when the earring forms a natural circle.

Figure 1

Circle Earring Legend

Legend

▭ Silver 3/0 Bugle Beads

● Crystal Teal 10/° Seed Beads

○ Silver 10/° Seed Beads

Variation

▭ Gold 3/0 Bugle Beads

● Black 11/° Seed Beads

SQUARE-TYPE EARRINGS

This is the basic foundation that will be used in the following eight earrings found in this section. This foundation may include any number of bugle beads.

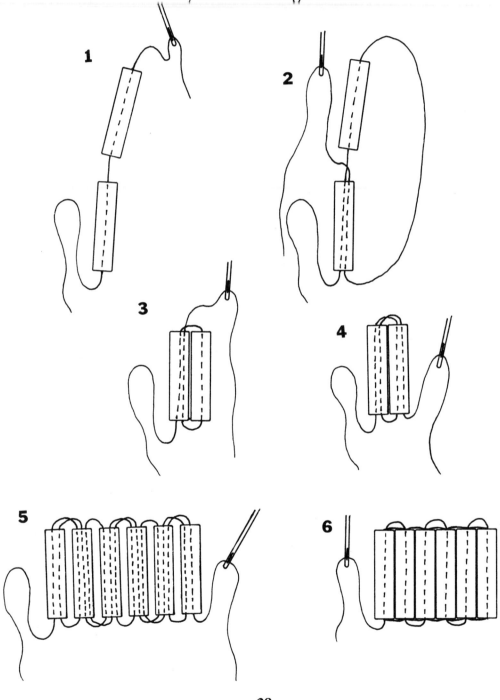

3 SQUARE EARRING

Materials Required

Size "A" Nymo Thread
Size 15/° Beading Needle
Size 4/0 Silver Rust Bugle Beads
Size 10/° Crystal Rust Seed Beads
Clear Fingernail Polish
Super Glue

Step 1 - With the thread measuring 2 1/2 yards in length, make a foundation, as shown on *Page 38*, of five bugle beads. After going back seed bead and attach at the junction thread between the first and second bugle beads (*Figure 1*). Continue with this technique until 4 seed beads are completed. With the thread coming up and out of the fourth seed bead, take the needle down through the fifth bugle bead and repeat attaching four seed beads on the other side and take the needle through the end bugle.

Figure 1

through your work for strength, thread on one

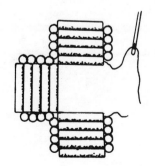

Figure 2

39

Repeat *Step 1* until you have completed two more foundation sections. Arrange these sections to look like *Figure 2*, by twisting them into position.

(*Note*: There are two methods of constructing this style of earring. One, which is used in these instructions, is to connect the foundations as you work. The other, illustrated and explained on *Page 42 - 43*, is to create the individual foundations and then connect them. With some experience you may choose the technique that is best for you.)

Step 2 - With the thread coming out of the first bugle bead on the third section to the right of your work, thread on one seed bead, pass the needle through the first bugle bead of the first section and pull the triangle closed. Thread on one seed bead and pass the needle through the first bugle bead of the second section. Repeat this step adding one seed bead between the second and third sections. Take the needle through the first bugles and the seed beads you just attached once more for strength, pulling the thread up tightly, snapping the seed beads into place between sections. *Figure 3* shows the placement of the seed beads between sections.

Figure 3

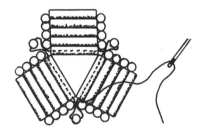

Step 3 - Begin working up through one

section (foundation) until the thread is coming out of the last bugle bead. Thread on six seed beads (or the number of beads it takes to be even in length with the bugle bead). Take the needle through the opposite end of the bugle bead, through the six seed beads, back through the bugle and through to the middle two seed beads of the six you have in place. Thread on six additional seed beads, go through the two seed beads of the middle six, go back up through the six you just threaded on, then through the middle two seed beads and the remained of the seed beads (*Figure 4*).

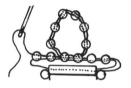

Figure 4

Now work the thread down through the bugle beads in the work, make a neat, secure knot, continue down through some more beads and cut off the excess thread. Continue with all of the tail-end threads in a similar manner.

FINISHING

Lay the work on a flat surface and put a drop of glue on the first seed bead that was added between the foundation sections. After this has dried, brush clear fingernail polish over the bugle sections and the seed beads in between. Allow 6 hours to dry completely.

3 Square Earring Legend

Legend

▭ Silver Rust 4/0 Bugle Beads

○ Crystal Rust 10/° Seed Beads

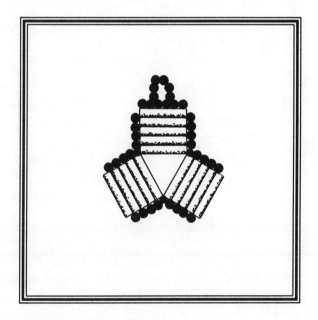

Variation

▭ Pink 3/0 Bugle Beads

● Pearl Pink 11/° Seed Beads

BUGLE STAR IN CIRCLE EARRING

Step 1 - Make a foundation (as shown on *Page 38*) of four bugle beads. In order to strengthen the work, go back through all of the bugle beads leaving the tail-end thread to the left of the work when finished.

Repeat this step until there are five groups

Figure 1

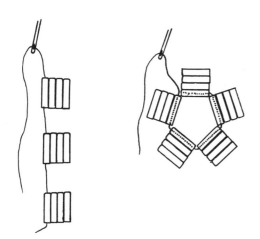

of four bugle bead foundations. When this is finished, pass the needle through the first bugle bead of each section as shown in *Figure 1*. Go through the first, or bottom, bugle bead a number of times for strength.

(*Note*: There are two methods of constructing this style of earring. One, which is used in these instructions, is to create the individual foundations and then connect them. The other is illustrated and explained in *Step One* on *Pages 39* and *40*. With some experience you may choose the technique that is best for you.)

Step 2 - Take the needle up and back

Figure 2

42

through the second bugle, thread on two seed beads, go through the corresponding hole in the second foundation, thread on two seed beads, and continue until you have gone through all five of the foundation groups. (*Figure 2*)

Come out where you began and then take the needle and go through the third bugle bead (going in the opposite direction). Thread on four seed beads between each bugle bead. When all of the groups have four seed beads between each of the bugle beads, go through the first four seed beads and the next bugle bead again, coming out at the left side of the third bugle bead. Go up through the fourth, or top, bugle bead. (*Figure 3*)

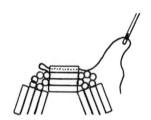

Figure 3

Step 3 - The ear-wire loop is to be made by threading on four seed beads (or however many it takes to fit across the bugle bead) and then going through the last bugle bead at the top (See *Figure 4*). Take the needle back through the seed beads and the bugle bead for strength. Now go through the first three seed beads on the top, thread on four seed beads, take the needle back into the second seed bead and then again through the third seed bead and then the four seed beads that form the loop. Go back through the second seed bead, through all of the seed beads in the top row and then work down through the project. Tie a nice neat knot between beads, take the thread down through the work and then clip off

Figure 4

the excess thread. Repeat this process with the tail-end thread.

FINISHING

Use clear fingernail polish on the bugle bead foundation and the first seed beads placed between the bugle beads. Allow four to six hours to dry on a flat surface.

43

Bugle Star in Circle Earring Legend

Legend

▭ Light Green 3/0 Bugle Beads

○ Gold 11/° Seed Beads

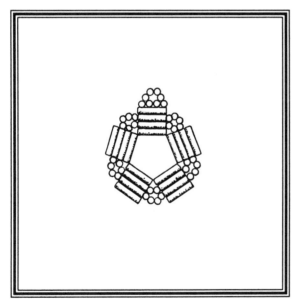

Variation

▭ Satin 3/0 Bugle Beads

○ Blue Lined Purple 11/°
Seed Beads

LARGE BUGLE RECTANGLE EARRING

Materials Required

Size "A" Nymo Thread
Size 15/° Beading Needle
Size Gold 4/0 or 5/0 Bugle Beads
Size Gold 11/° Seed Beads
Clear Fingernail Polish

Step 1 - Make a foundation of five bugle beads as shown on *Page 38*. Finish threading back through the foundation for strength and when at the bottom of the second bugle bead, tie a knot with the tail-end thread and the needle thread. Pass the needle thread up through the

following the course through the first and fifth bugle beads in the foundation. This will be a square movement. Pull the thread tightly, keeping the bugle beads lined up neatly on the top and bottom of the center foundation.

Step 2 - Begin at one end bugle and add on four bugle beads as if making another foundation. When one section is completed, you go

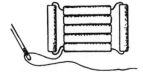

Figure 1

first bugle bead. Put the tail-end thread on another needle and work the thread back through the work. Clip off any excess thread. Thread on one bugle bead and take the needle down the end bugle bead as shown in *Figure 1*. Thread on another (the seventh) bugle bead.

Go back through the sixth and seventh bugle beads (those added to the foundation),

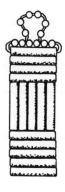

Figure 2

45

back through to stengthen, passing through the foundation bugle beads and up through the other bugle bead at the other end to begin the foundation process again, adding on just three bugle beads.

Step 3 - When finished with the three additional bugle beads, go through them to strengthen. Go through the center section (with an up and down movement), then back through the top 4 bugle beads again, coming out of the fourth bugle bead. You will then thread on eight seed beads (or however many it takes to be even in length with the bugle). Go back through the last bugle bead and through the seed beads until you reach the center two seed beads. Come out and thread on six seed beads, taking the needle back through the center two seed beads, up through the six seed bead loop, and through the remaining seed beads on the top of the bugle. Tie a nice neat knot, work down through the beads and then clip off any excess thread. (*Figure 2*)

FINISHING

Place the work on a flat surface. Brush clear fingernail polish over all of the bugles and then allow four to six hours to dry.

OPTION

As pictured on the next page, this is a three bugle bead foundation, using a size 3/0 bugle bead and 11/° seed beads. At the ear wire loop, it will take approximately five seed beads across the top and six beads to form the loop. With these changes, follow the instructions above.

Large Bugle Rectangle Earring Legend

Legend

▭ Gold 5/0 Bugle Beads

○ Gold 11/° Seed Beads

Option/Variation

▭ Orange 3/0 Bugle Beads

● Luster Orange 11/° Seed Beads

SMALL BUGLE BASE EARRING

Materials Required

Size "A" Nymo Thread
Size 15/° Beading Needle
Size 3/0 Bugle Beads
Black
Silver Pink
Size 12/° Seed Beads
Pink
Metal Pink
Black
Clear Fingernail Polish

Step 1 - Make a foundation of four bugle beads as shown on *Page 38*. With the needle coming out of the left-hand side of the top bugle bead, add six seed beads (or as many as it takes

Figure 1

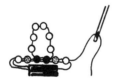

to be even with the bugle bead), then go back through the top bugle bead and out of the right side as shown in *Figure 1*. Proceed back through the first four seed beads, add six seed beads and then go down through the third seed bead and

through the rest of the seed beads at the top (you may want to go through the loop again for some added strength).

Step 2 - In a back and forth motion, work down to the fifth, or bottom, bugle bead. Thread on five seed beads, one bugle bead, twenty-five seed beads, one bugle bead and five seed beads (look at the *Legend* for the proper sequence). Then go through the bottom bugle bead in the foundation. Go back through the five seed beads and the bugle bead in the dangle and then add seventeen seed beads, go back through the bugle bead and then the five seed beads, into the fifth bugle bead in the foundation and then up and through the fourth bugle bead (second from the bottom).

Step 3 - With the thread coming out of the fourth bugle bead add five seed beads, one bugle bead and then fifty seed beads, one bugle bead and five seed beads and back through the fourth bugle bead. Then continue through the first five seed beads and the bugle beads and then add thirty-seven seed beads, then through the bugle bead and the top five seed beads and then back into the foundation (*Figure 2* will give you an idea of the form to create).

FINISHING

Work through the foundation, make a knot, work through the project and then clip off any excess thread. Lay the work on a flat surface and brush on clear fingernail polish on the bugle bead foundation and the first few beads that begin the loops at the sides. Allow the earring four to six hours to dry completely.

Figure 2

OPTION

You may use size 3/0 bugle beads with a size 11/° seed beads for a more proportional look.

Small Bugle Base Earring Legend

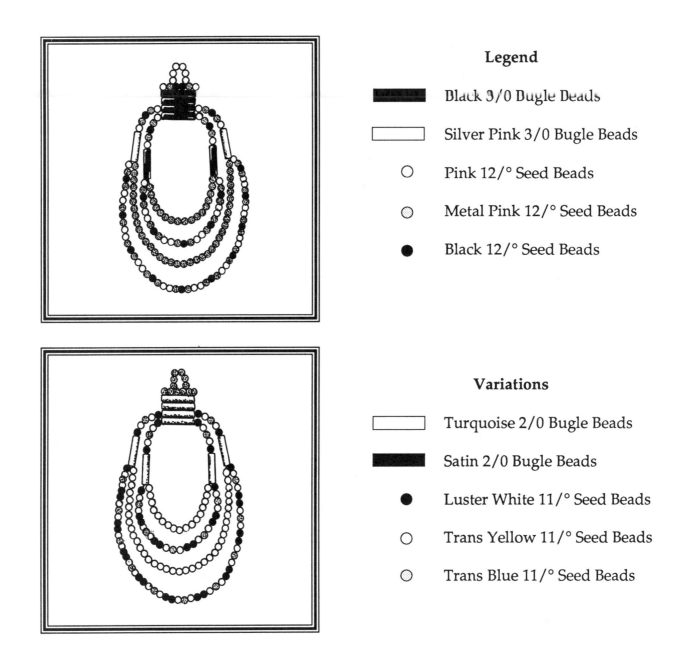

Legend

▬▬▬ Black 3/0 Bugle Beads

▭ Silver Pink 3/0 Bugle Beads

○ Pink 12/° Seed Beads

◉ Metal Pink 12/° Seed Beads

● Black 12/° Seed Beads

Variations

▭ Turquoise 2/0 Bugle Beads

▬▬▬ Satin 2/0 Bugle Beads

● Luster White 11/° Seed Beads

○ Trans Yellow 11/° Seed Beads

◉ Trans Blue 11/° Seed Beads

FIVE BUGLE BASE EARRING

Materials Required

Size "A" Nymo Thread
Size 15/° Beading Needle
Size 4/0 Gold Bugle Beads
Size 3/0 Silver Bugle Beads
Size 5/0 Silver Bugle Beads
Size 11/° Seed Beads
Gold
Silver
Clear Fingernail Polish

Step 1 - Make a foundation of five large (4/0) Bugle Beads as shown and illustrated on *Page 38*. After going back through the foundation for strengthening, come out of the top bugle bead and add three gold seed beads, two silver seed beads, three gold seed beads and then go back through the top bugle bead in the foundation. Proceed back through the first gold seed beads and then the two silver ones, add six silver seed beads, go back through the two silver seed beads on the top row and then again through the six silver seed beads in the loop (for strengthening). Then go back through the two silver seed beads and the last three gold seed beads and then back through the top bugle bead (*Figure 1*).

Step 2 - Work your way down through the foundation bugle beads in a back and forth motion until you reach the bottom, or fifth, bugle bead. After going through the bottom bugle bead, (following the Legend) thread on five seed beads, one 5/0 bugle bead, twenty-six seed beads, one 5/0 bugle bead, five seed beads and then back through the bottom bugle bead in the foundation. Then go back through the first five seed beads and the 5/0 bugle bead and then thread on twenty seed beads, go back through the 5/0 bugle bead on the other side, then the five seed beads and back through the fifth bugle bead and then up and through the fourth bugle bead in the foundation. (*Figure 2*)

Figure 2

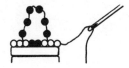

Figure 1

Step 3 - After going through the fourth bugle bead (second from the bottom) in the foundation row (following the *Legend* for the proper color sequence), thread on seven seed beads, one 5/0 bugle bead, three seed beads, one 3/0 bugle bead, one seed bead, one 3/0 bugle bead, seventeen seed beads, one 3/0 bugle bead, one seed bead, one 3/0 bugle bead, three seed beads, one 5/0 bugle bead, seven seed beads and then go through the fourth bugle bead in the foundation again. Then proceed back through the seed beads, bugle bead, seed beads, bugle bead, seed beads, bugle bead and then thread on fifteen seed beads. Now go back up through the bugle bead, seed beads, bugle bead, seed beads, 5/0 bugle bead and seed beads on the other side and back through the fourth bugle bead in the foundation row. See *Figure 3* for an illustration of the completed earring.

Step 4 - Work your way to the tail-end thread, tie a small neat knot and then continue working through the beads and cut off the excess thread. Do the same with the tail-end thread.

FINISHING

Lay the earring on a flat surface and brush on clear fingernail polish on the bugle foundation only. Allow to dry for four to six hours.

OPTION

The variation shown on the next page is but one of many options that may be made from the instructions included above. By changing the size of the bugle beads and seed beads, many beautiful and distinctive earrings are possible.

Figure 3

Five Bugle Base Earring Legend

Legend

▭	Gold 4/0 Bugle Beads
▬	Silver 3/0 Bugle Beads
▨	Silver 5/0 Bugle Beads
○	Gold 11/° Seed Beads
●	Silver 11/° Seed Beads

Variation

▭	Silver 3/0 Bugle Beads
▨	Satin 2/0 Bugle Beads
▬	Royal Blue 7/8" Bugle Beads
●	Blue-Lined Purple 11/° Beads
○	Crystal 11/° Seed Beads

SEVEN BUGLE BASE EARRING

Materials Required
Size "A" Nymo Thread
Size 15/° Beading Needle
Size 4/0 Rust Bugle Beads
Size 10/° 3-Cut Seed Beads
Rust
Crystal
Clear Fingernail Polish

Step 1 - Make a foundation of five bugle beads as shown on *Page 38*. After strengthening the foundation, with the thread going out of the first bugle bead, add one bugle bead and go back through the fifth bugle bead, add one bugle bead and then go back through the first bugle bead, thus adding one bugle bead on each side of the foundation. Follow this procedure again to add strength. (*Figure 1*)

Figure 2

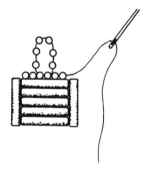

Step 2 - Come out of the left side of the first bugle bead in the foundation and thread on six seed beads (or the number required to go across the top bugle bead) and then go back through the first bugle bead. Then go back through the first four seed beads across the top, add six seed beads, go back through the third seed bead, through the fourth again, through the six seed beads in the loop and back into the third seed bead (*Figure 2*). Continue through the rest of the seed beads at the top and then

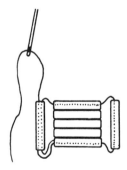

Figure 1

54

Figure 3
Figure 5

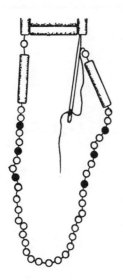

through the top bugle bead in the foundation.

Step 3 - Now take the needle down through the bugle bead on the left side of the foundation, add one seed bead, one bugle bead, thirty-eight seed beads (following the *Legend* for the longest loop), one bugle bead, one seed bead and then back up through the bugle bead on the right side of the foundation. (*Figure 3*)

Step 4 - Go through the top, or first, bugle bead, then through the second down, then the third, fourth and through the fifth, or bottom bugle bead. The needle will be coming out on the left side (*Figure 4*). Go through the seed bead at the bottom of the side bugle bead, then down through the bottom bugle bead at the side dangle and then thread on thirty-six seed beads. Go

back up through the bottom side bugle bead on the other side, through the seed bead and then through the bottom, or fifth, bugle bead.

Step 5 - After going through the bottom bugle bead, go back through the seed bead at the bottom of the top side bugle, then through the bottom bugle bead and then string on thirty-two seed beads. Then back through the bottom bugle bead on the right side, through the seed bead and then work the thread through the work.

FINISHING

After working through the work, make a knot between beads and then continue through the work to a point where you can cut off the excess thread. Do the same thing on the tail-end thread. Place the earring on a flat surface and brush on clear fingernail polish on the foundation and side bugle beads only. Then allow the project to dry completely for four to six hours.

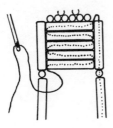

Figure 4

55

Seven Bugle Base Earring Legend

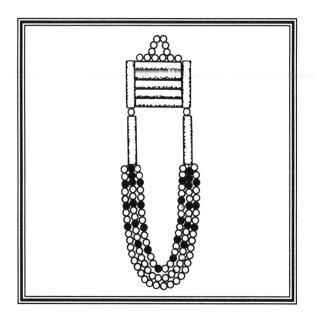

Legend

▭ Rust 4/0 Bugle Beads

○ Rust 10/° 3-Cut Seed Beads

● Crystal 10/° 3-Cut Seed Beads

Variation

▬ Dark Blue 3/0 Bugle Beads

● Luster White 11/° Seed Beads

○ White Lined Blue 11/° Beads

TEN BUGLE BASE EARRING

Materials Required

Size "A" Nymo Thread
Size 15/° Beading Needle
Size 4/0 Silver Teal Bugle Beads
Size Teal 10/° 3-Cut Seed Beads
Size Crystal 10/° Seed Beads
Clear Fingernail Polish

Step 1 - First make a foundation of six bugle beads as shown and illustrated on *Page 38*. Go back through the bugle bead foundation to add some strength and finish so that the thread is coming out of the top left-hand side of the top bugle bead in the foundation. Thread on one bugle bead, one seed bead and go through the fifth, second from the bottom, bugle bead. Thread on one seed bead, one bugle bead and then go back through the first (top) bugle bead in the foundation (*Figure 1*). Go through all of the bugles in the earring in a square movement again until all of the bugles are lined up correctly, pulling the thread taut.

Figure 1

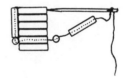

Figure 2

Step 2 - To the bugle bead on the left side, add another bugle bead in the same way you made the foundation. Then work your way through the foundation to the right side and, in the same way, add a bugle bead. You should have two bugle beads on each side of the center six foundation bugle beads. In order to make the following instructions easier, we will number the outside, vertical bugle beads as 1, 2, 3

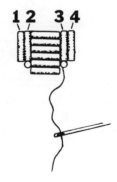

57

and 4 from left to right. (*Figure 2*)

Figure 3

Step 3 - After adding the two bugles to each side, the thread should be coming down out of Number 3 and through the seed bead at the bottom of that bugle bead. Thread on one seed bead, one bugle bead, then twenty-one seed beads, one bugle bead, one seed bead, go through the seed bead at the bottom on Number 2, then up through Number 2 and down through Number 1. Thread on three seed beads, one bugle bead, then forty seed beads, one bugle bead, three seed beads and then go up through Number 4.

Step 4 - Now take the needle down through Number 3, go through the two seed beads and the bugle bead and then thread on sixteen seed beads and go up through the bugle bead and seed beads at the bottom of Number 2, through Number 2 and then down through Number 1. Continue through the three seed beads and the bugle bead and then thread on thirty-one seed beads and then up through the bugle bead, seed beads and Number 4.

Step 5 - There are now two rows in place on each dangle. Take the needle down through Number 3, the seed beads, the bugle bead and then thread on eleven seed beads, then up through the bugle bead, seed beads and then Number 2. For the final row, go down through Number 1, the seed beads and the bugle bead and then thread on twenty-seven seed beads and finish by going up through the bugle bead, seed beads and then Number 4.

Step 6 - The final step before finishing is to add the ear-wire loop to the top. Take the needle back down into Number 3 and through the first seed bead. Come out and go through the bottom, or sixth, bugle bead in the foundation row, then through the fifth, etc., working your way up through the foundation bugle beads. You will emerge at the right side of the top, or first, bugle bead.

Thread on six seed beads (or the number

it takes to run the length of the top bugle bead) and then, from left to right, go through the top bugle bead(*Figure 3*). Now go back through the first four seed beads, thread on six seed beads and then go back through the seed beads at the top entering at the third seed bead from the right. Go back through the work until you can make a knot between beads, then continue through the work and then then clip off any excess thread. Do the same with any tail-end threads.

FINISHING

Lay the earring on a flat surface and brush on clear fingernail polish on the bugle bead foundation only. Allow to dry completely; usually four to six hours.

OPTIONS

The ear-wire loop, for those experienced in making the earrings shown in the preceeding pages, might be added after completing the initial six bead foundation. However, that does expose the loop to a great deal of abuse while making the rest of the earring.

Ten Bugle Base Legend

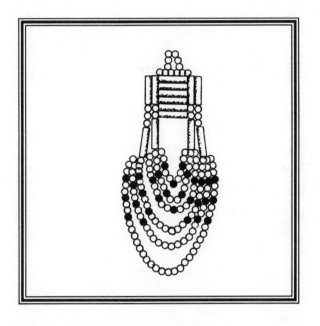

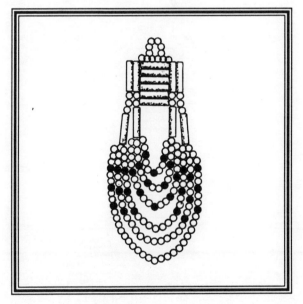

Legend

▭	Silver Teal 4/0 Bugle Beads
○	Teal 10/° 3-Cut Seed Beads
●	Crystal 10/° 3-Cut Seed Beads

Variation

▭	Gold 3/0 Bugle Beads
○	Dark Purple 11/° Seed Beads
●	Luster Opal 11/° Seed Beads

ONE DIMENSIONAL CUBE EARRING

Materials Required

Size "A" Nymo Thread
Size 15/° Beading Needle
Size 3/0 Crystal Bugle Beads
Size 11/° Crystal Seed Beads
Clear Fingernail Polish

As mentioned in the Introduction, bugle and seed beads are made by hand and there is often variations in size in every package or hank. It is very important, especially with this project, to make sure that all of your bugle beads are exactly the same size in length and width.

Figure 1

Step 1 - Begin by making a foundation using five bugle beads as shown on *Page 38*. Finish by threading back through the foundation for strength and when at the bottom of the second bugle bead, tie a neat knot with the tail-end thread and the needle thread. Pass the needle thread up through the first bugle bead - do not cut. Put the tail-end thread on another needle and work the thread back through the work. Clip off any excess thread. On the needle thread, string on one bugle bead and take the needle down the end bugle bead as shown in *Figure 1*.

Figure 2

Go back through the sixth and seventh bugle beads (those added to the foundation), following the course through the first and fifth bugle beads in the foundation. This will be a square movement. Pull the thread tightly, keeping the bugle beads lined up neatly on the top and bottom of the center foundation.

Step 2 - Begin at one end bugle and add on four bugle beads as if making another foundation. When one section is completed, go back through to strengthen, passing through the foundation bugle beads and up through the other bugle bead at the other end to begin the foundation process again, this time adding four bugle beads. Each foundation section in this project will have five bugle beads.

Step 3 - When finished with the four additional bugle beads, go through the center foundation bugle beads, then back through the section just finished (the top) and turn your work so that the needle is coming out of the left side of the top bugle bead.

Step 4 - You then thread on eight seed beads (or however many it takes to be even in length with the bugle). Go back through the last bugle bead and through the seed beads again until you reach the center two seed beads. Come out and thread on six seed beads, take the needle back through the center two seed beads, up through the six seed bead loop, and then on through the remaining seed beads on the top of the bugle and on through the top bugle bead. (Figure 2)

Step 5 - You should have the thread coming out of the first (top) bugle bead. Turn

your work and thread on one bugle bead to the right of the first set of bugle beads that include the ear-wire loop. Then go through the fifth bugle bead (bottom of this section), thread on one bugle bead to the left and go back through the top bugle bead as shown in Figure 3.

Step 6 - Thread back in a square motion to strengthen and keep the bugle beads even. To one side, thread on bugles as in creating a foundation. When a five bugle bead section has been completed, thread back through in an up and down motion, going through the appropriate bugle beads in the center, and over to and up through the bugle bead on the other side. Repeat making a five bugle bead foundation on that side so that the work now looks like a "T" as shown in Figure 4. Tie a knot with the needle thread between beads, work the thread through some more beads and then clip off the excess.

Figure 4

Step 7 - At one of the junction points (shown on Figure 4), tie on a new thread 1 1/2 yards in length, leaving a tail-end thread measuring about six inches long. Pass the needle through the first bugle bead of the bottom-center section. Put the tail-end thread on another needle, pass through the work and then clip off any excess.

Step 8 - With the needle coming out of the top bugle bead in the bottom-center section, repeat Steps 5 and 6. When this is completed, the

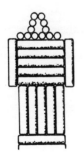

Figure 3

61

work should look like that shown in *Figure 5*.

Step 9 - Attach a new thread (2 yards long) at the top right junction (shown in *Figure 5*). Finish the tail-end thread in the manner described above. Thread on one bugle bead. Pass the needle over to and up through the top right end bugle bead (*Figure 6*). Go through the fourth bugle bead next to it and back down the bugle you threaded into place. Thread on another bugle bead and continue working as in making a five bugle bead foundation. Go back to strengthen and when finished, take the needle back through to the fifth bugle bead. Thread should come out at the bottom. Pass the needle through the first bugle bead of the bottom right section, working through this section to the fourth bugle bead. Take the needle over and through the fifth bugle bead. The thread should be at the bottom of this last bugle bead. Take the needle through the second bugle bead of the bottom right section then work through, coming out of the last bugle bead and go over and down through the fifth bugle again. This right center section is now attached to the top right and bottom right sections.

Step 10 - Work through the center five

bugle beads. Thread should come up through the first bugle bead in the center section. Thread on one bugle bead. Take the needle over to and through the first bugle bead of the top left section. Go down the second bugle bead and back through the bugle you previously threaded on. Turn the work so that the bugle is at your left. Continue working the foundation process and then repeat the directions in *Step 9* to make sure that this final section is attached to the top left and bottom left sections.

FINISHING

Straighten the work out on a flat surface. Liberally brush clear fingernail polish over each section, following in the direction that the bugle beads run. Allow to dry overnight or eight to ten hours.

OPTION

As shown in the *variation*, on the next page, this earring may be made with a three bugle bead base.

Figure 5

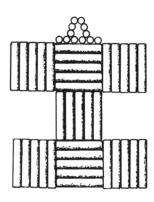

Figure 6

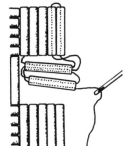
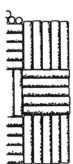

62

One Dimensional Cube Earring Legend

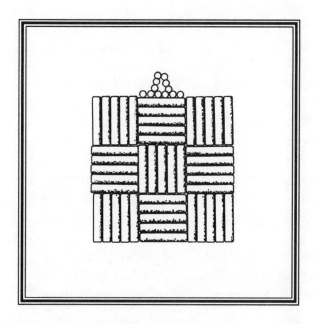

Legend

▭   Crystal 4/0 Bugle Beads

○   Crystal 11/° Seed Beads

Variation

▬   Dark Blue 3/0 Bugle Beads

▭   Gold 3/0 Bugle Bead

○   Crystal 11/° Seed Bead

The Technique of
North American Indian Beadwork
by Monte Smith

This informative and easy to read book was written by noted author and editor Monte Smith and contains complete instructions on every facet of doing Indian beadwork.

Included is information on selecting beads; materials used (and how to use them); designs, with a special emphasis on Tribal differences; step-by-step instructions on how to make a loom, doing loom work and the variations of loom work; applique stitches including the lazy stitch, "Crow" stitch, running stitch, spot stitch, and return stitch; bead wrapping and peyote stitch; how to make rosettes; making beaded necklaces; and, a special section on beadwork edging. There is also a section of notes, a selected bibliography and an index.

The book features examples and photos of beadwork from 1835 to the present time from twenty-three Tribes. A book of 106 pages with 200 illustrations in black/white and color.

Anyone interested in the craft work of the North American Indian will profit from owning this fine book.

$9.95 in Paperback << >> $15.95 in Hardbound

Indian Clothing of the Great Lakes:
1740 - 1840
by Sheryl Hartman

Illustrated by Greg Hudson and Joe Lee. An exciting new book that fills a void in the literature of Native American crafts. The author gives an explanation, illustrations, and patterns for the woman's strap dress, leggings, shirts, caped shirt, chamise, jacket and Canadian dress. Also included are men's hairstyles and adornment, head coverings, breechclout, leggings, shirt, trade coat and blanket stroud. In addition, there is information on quilts, knife sheaths, moosehair embroidery, trade beads, trade silver, body painting, tattooing and finger weaving.

Included are articles on the history of finger weaving by Dick Carney, finger weaving by Mae Ring and the history of trade silver by Chuck Leonard.

All aspects of Indian clothing and adornment are covered for the area of the Great Lakes Indian Nations. This is a fine book with patterns that are easy to follow.

$9.95 in Paperback